The 2004
Commemorative
Stamp
Yearbook

UNITED STATES POSTAL SERVICE

MARTIN JOHNSON HEADE | USA 37

2004

An Imprint of HarperCollins *Publishers*

Other books available from the United States Postal Service:

THE 2003 COMMEMORATIVE STAMP YEARBOOK

THE POSTAL SERVICE GUIDE TO U.S. STAMPS
31st Edition

HarperCollins books may be purchased for educational, business, or sales promotional use.
For information please write: Special Markets Department, HarperCollins Publishers Inc.,
10 East 53rd Street, New York, NY 10022.

Library of Congress Cataloging-in-Publication Data has been applied for.
ISBN: 0-06-052823-0

Contents

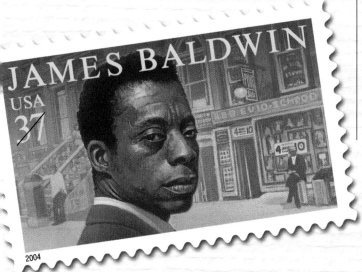

Introduction
  by Kitty Carlisle Hart 4
Lunar New Year:
  Year of the Monkey 6
Black Heritage:
  Paul Robeson 8
Love: Candy Hearts 10
Theodor Seuss Geisel 12
Garden Blossoms 14
U.S. Air Force Academy 16
Legends of Hollywood:
  John Wayne 18
Henry Mancini 20
Lewis & Clark 22
American Choreographers 26
Isamu Noguchi 30
National World War II Memorial . . . 32

The Art of Disney:
  Friendship 34
2004 Olympic Games:
  Athens, Greece 36
R. Buckminster Fuller 38
Literary Arts:
  James Baldwin 40
American Treasures:
  Martin Johnson Heade 42
USS Constellation 44
Art of the American Indian 46
Cloudscapes 50
Sickle Cell Disease:
  Awareness 52
Moss Hart 54
Nature of America:
  Pacific Coral Reef 56
Holiday Celebrations:
  Hanukkah and Kwanzaa 58
Holiday Ornaments and Christmas . . 60
Photo Credits 62
Acknowledgments 64

Introduction

by Kitty Carlisle Hart

As a lifelong advocate of the arts, I have spent much of my career spreading the word that experiencing dance, theater, music, and the visual arts is one of the finest ways to nourish the soul. For that reason I am quite pleased to present this edition of the *Commemorative Stamp Yearbook*, especially during a year in which stamps celebrate the arts and their importance in our national life.

In 1999, I had the honor of participating in the ceremony for the Broadway Songwriters stamps. My first love has always been the musical theater, and I consider it a privilege to have witnessed firsthand the golden age of Broadway, when so many wonderful composers gave us timeless songs. It was a true pleasure to take part in the commemoration of these talented figures, whose works delight us still.

This year, the stamp program again holds special meaning for me. Not only is the Postal Service honoring an acclaimed dramatist and director, but that honoree also happens to be my late husband, Moss Hart, who loved with all his heart the dreams and drama of Broadway. When I was shown the stamp artwork created by Tim O'Brien, I was profoundly moved. Being commemorated on a stamp is a rare distinction and my happiness at seeing Moss recognized for his role in American culture is an emotion I can scarcely describe in words.

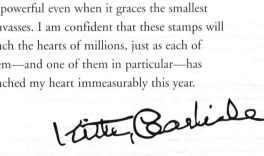

In the pages that follow, Mr. O'Brien and other talented professionals tell the stories behind this year's stamps, shedding light on the ins and outs of the creative process. These designers, artists, and photographers are clearly aware of their shared responsibility, which is to ensure that stamps connect powerfully with those who see them. I believe that in the end, that connection is the goal of all great art.

As this *Stamp Yearbook* confirms, art can be powerful even when it graces the smallest canvasses. I am confident that these stamps will touch the hearts of millions, just as each of them—and one of them in particular—has touched my heart immeasurably this year.

ABOVE: Kitty Carlisle Hart and Moss Hart in London, 1956. FACING PAGE: Well known as a lifelong advocate of the arts, Kitty Carlisle Hart served as chairman of the New York State Council on the Arts from 1976 until 1996, and she received the National Medal of the Arts in 1991.

Year of the Monkey

hen Honolulu-based graphic artist Clarence Lee created his first Lunar New Year stamp in 1992, he crafted his design around a paper-cut animal shape, a nod to tradition that has made the twelve stamps in this series among the most instantly recognizable in recent years.

"The paper-cut motif turned out to be a wonderful device," Lee says. "This graphic treatment goes back 2,000 years to ancient China, and here it provided a strong visual link between all of the stamps."

This year, as the Postal Service concludes the series during the Year of the Monkey, Lee finds himself thinking about the public's overwhelmingly positive reaction to all of the Lunar New Year stamps. "I have met so many fine people," he says, "and I've learned that stamp design is practically a universal language."

In addition, Lee says that his rediscovery of Asian-American history through stamp design has left him not only proud of his heritage, but also grateful for such a rare artistic opportunity.

"I need to thank many people," he says, "but primarily my parents, because they allowed me to pursue my passion for art even though most Chinese in my generation were pressured to pursue careers in more secure professions such as law, medicine, engineering, or business. To let me pursue art and design was very unusual."

As a designer for more than 40 years, Lee has created everything from corporate logos to posters for international exhibitions, but he says that the positive response to his designs for the Lunar New Year stamps has been one of the most fulfilling experiences of his career.

"In the end," he says, "my life has changed, because my smallest project has provided me with the largest satisfaction."

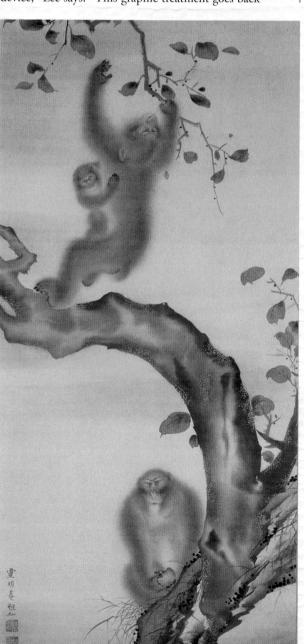

Place and Date of Issue . . . . **San Francisco, CA, January 13, 2004**
Art Director . . . . **Terrence W. McCaffrey**
Designer and Artist . . . . **Clarence Lee**

LEFT: *A monkey family graces a beautiful Japanese drawing.* ABOVE: *A delightful early 19th-century drawing of a capuchin monkey.* FACING PAGE: *A painting of a colobus monkey by Lizzie Riches.*

Paul Robeson

With his powerful voice and his uncompromising commitment to social justice, Paul Robeson was a man ahead of his time. This 27th stamp in the Black Heritage series commemorates Robeson for his accomplishments as an actor, singer, activist, and athlete—and for being one of the most fascinating Americans of the last century.

Robeson's talents were evident at an early age. Born in Princeton, New Jersey, in 1898, he was a brilliant student and athlete who became the third African American to attend Rutgers College, graduating in 1919 as class valedictorian and an All-American football player. After earning a law degree from Columbia University, Robeson seemed destined for a future as an attorney, but when a white secretary at a law firm refused to take dictation from him, he devoted himself full-time to performing.

Robeson was more than just another American performer; he was a phenomenon. Whether playing the lead in Eugene O'Neill plays, interpreting the title character of Shakespeare's *Othello*, or starring in movies such as *The Emperor Jones* and *The Proud Valley*, he brought presence, dignity, and power to every

role. As a singer, Robeson gave the world the definitive rendition of "Ol' Man River," and his concerts popularized spirituals as a legitimate American art form. His unforgettable voice—a dramatic, resonant baritone—lent authority to his controversial role as an activist, from his commitment to labor and peace movements to his advocacy for civil rights.

To exemplify the essential humanity of this talented figure, art director Richard Sheaff chose a photograph that shows a smiling Robeson during the prime of his career. Although the photographer is unknown, an inscription on the print obtained by the U.S. Postal Service offered significant clues. Found among Robeson's papers, the print was inscribed to Annette and Basil Zarov and dated February 8, 1943.

Postal Service researchers soon learned that Basil Zarov had been a Montreal-based photojournalist whose wide-ranging subjects included scenes from World War II, United Nations missions in Africa, and portraits of famous individuals made in collaboration with his wife Annette. Unfortunately, a large portion of Zarov's collection was lost, but the surviving pieces—including 12,000 negatives and 300 prints—are now in the National Archives of Canada.

Although no documentation accompanied this print, Robeson's own handwriting on the photograph provided a revealing clue about its origin and offered assurance that he would have approved of its use. In the lower left corner of the print, just above Robeson's signature, is his own unambiguous assessment of the Zarovs' work: "The pictures were beautiful."

■

Place and Date of Issue . . . . **Princeton, NJ, January 20, 2004**

Art Director and Designer . . . . **Richard Sheaff**

FACING PAGE: *Paul Robeson thrilled theater audiences in the title role of Eugene O'Neill's* The Emperor Jones, *reprising the role in the 1933 film version (*ABOVE*).* CENTER: *The musical* Show Boat *gave the world Robeson's powerful rendition of the song "Ol' Man River."*

LOVE
Candy Hearts

Each Love stamp represents an opportunity for an artist to explore a variation on a familiar and universal theme. When Michael Osborne decided to base the design for this year's stamp around candy hearts, he wasn't sure if he had been struck by genuine inspiration—or if he was subconsciously remembering a stamp design he had seen somewhere else.

"It was one of those ideas where you just slap yourself on the forehead," he says, laughing. "I did some research to make sure the idea hadn't already been used on a stamp. It seemed like such an obvious concept that I was amazed it hadn't been done before."

The Candy Hearts stamp is sure to receive widespread use on millions of envelopes, and Osborne points out that it has already found an especially receptive audience with NECCO, the Massachusetts-based company that manufactures the famous confections shown on the stamp.

While attending the first-day ceremony, Osborne discovered that NECCO maintains the popularity of its iconic treats by making annual changes to some of the messages that appear on them.

"The company creates several new sayings each year," he explains. "The current CEO likes to base them around a worthy cause or organization, and in 2004 it was the Make-A-Wish Foundation."

This year, however, NECCO made room for a special addition to their roster of sweet sayings: a candy heart that featured the affectionate phrase shown on the stamp.

"That was a really great honor," Osborne says. "After all, how many artists get to see their work reflected on a world-renowned treat?"

◼

Place and Date of Issue . . . . **Boston, MA, January 14, 2004**

Art Director . . . . **Ethel Kessler**

Designer . . . . **Michael Osborne**

Theodor Seuss Geisel

Before art director Carl T. Herrman designed this stamp to commemorate the 100th birthday of Theodor Seuss Geisel, he did what any Seussian scholar would do: he went to his local library.

"I checked out all of the Dr. Seuss books that they had," he says. "I didn't feel that only a portrait of him would be sufficient to convey the joy he brought to children through his clever books and flamboyant drawings." Herrman immersed himself in the fantastic world of the Pulitzer Prize–winning author and illustrator, selecting several colorful characters to appear alongside their creator on the stamp.

Another library close to Herrman's home also proved to be an invaluable resource: the Geisel Library at the University of California, San Diego.

"The library was endowed by Mrs. Geisel," Herrman explains, "and it was one of the most magnificent campus libraries I've ever seen. Their collection contained original drawings, sketches, proofs, notebooks, photographs, and memorabilia covering the life of Dr. Seuss from his high school activities in 1919 until his death in 1991. The director of the collection was able to find all of the originals that I needed for the stamp."

After acquiring copies of the original sketches, Herrman surrounded a 1987 photograph of Dr. Seuss with six colorful characters: The Cat in the

Dr. Seuss, who brought countless zany characters to life, also helped millions of children learn to read.

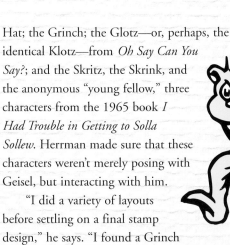

Hat; the Grinch; the Glotz—or, perhaps, the identical Klotz—from *Oh Say Can You Say?*; and the Skritz, the Skrink, and the anonymous "young fellow," three characters from the 1965 book *I Had Trouble in Getting to Solla Sollew.* Herrman made sure that these characters weren't merely posing with Geisel, but interacting with him.

"I did a variety of layouts before settling on a final stamp design," he says. "I found a Grinch with an extended hand, so I made it look like he was playfully tugging on Dr. Seuss's bow tie. The creature from the title page of *Oh Say Can You Say?* is teetering on some wobbly blue pilings, and his eye lines up perfectly to stare into Dr. Seuss's eye."

Meanwhile, one famous Seussian creation became the perfect observer of the whole colorful spectacle, and his bemused smile sums up the happiness that Theodor Geisel brought to millions of children.

"The Cat in the Hat fit perfectly to the left of the portrait," says Herrman, "and he looks like he's enjoying the entire scene."

■

Place and Date of Issue . . . . **La Jolla, CA, March 2, 2004**
Art Director and Designer . . . . **Carl T. Herrman**

Garden Blossoms

Drawings of beautiful flowers never go out of style. Even so, the artists who created the artwork for these two new stamps could never have imagined that their designs would blossom again more than a century later.

"Victorian flowers have been very popular on past stamps," says art director Richard Sheaff, who maintains an enormous collection of paper ephemera. "I was asked to be on the alert to see if I could find something similar for these new stamps that would be used for special occasions."

For the 37-cent stamp, which features a bouquet of white lilacs and pink roses, Sheaff decided to use a reproduction of a chromolithograph probably printed in Germany at the end of the 19th century.

"It's from a die-cut piece of scrap," Sheaff says. "It's an example of something that was very popular at that time. People would collect them and glue them into scrapbooks

 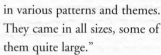

in various patterns and themes. They came in all sizes, some of them quite large."

The 60-cent stamp, featuring a botanical illustration of five varieties of simple pink roses, reproduces a chromolithograph created from a drawing by English artist Anne Pratt. The drawing was one of hundreds originally published in a five-volume set of Pratt's illustrations at the end of the 19th century.

Making sure that the two stamps complemented each other was a priority for Sheaff, who knew that people will be using the 60-cent stamp to send wedding invitations and the 37-cent stamps for their response cards.

"The book was full of flower illustrations," he says, "but the one we're using on this stamp turned out to be a nice match for the 37-cent artwork. Even though they come from different sources, they really look like they belong together."

◼

Place and Date of Issue . . . . **New York, NY, March 4, 2004**
Art Director and Designer . . . . **Richard Sheaff**

U.S. Air Force Academy

"The U.S. Air Force Academy is one of the most inspiring places on the planet," says Philip Handleman, who specializes in photographing aviation-related subjects. For this stamp commemorating the 50th anniversary of the academy, Handleman made several early-morning trips to the campus near Colorado Springs, Colorado, where one daily ritual left him deeply moved.

"In sight of the black granite War Memorial inscribed with the names of academy graduates who have fallen in combat, the honor guard members raise the American flag against the backdrop of rousing music and then, in unison and totally oblivious to any camera that might be clicking away, they stand erect, eyes focused aloft, and crisply salute the symbol of their country. How best to capture this magnificent spirit in a photograph, how to appropriately portray this pervasive ethic of duty and honor in a single image, became my mandate."

After viewing the academy from every conceivable angle, Handleman found his perfect shot one morning outside the Cadet Chapel, the architectural centerpiece of the campus.

"I have always believed that humankind is at its noblest when reaching for the heavens," he says, "and here we were, peering skyward next to the academy's identifying landmark, as if something beckoned." Handleman discovered an uncommon perspective at the southeastern corner of the chapel, and the resulting photograph became the basis for this stamp.

"We wanted to include an Air Force airplane zooming over the Cadet Chapel," Handleman adds, "but regulations forbade aircraft from swooping down to an altitude where they would be anything more than mere specks in the sky. Rather than abandoning the idea completely, as an acknowledgement of the aviation aspect a few columns of contrails were superimposed across the sky."

Though passionate about aviation, Handleman is nonetheless solemn when he ponders his role in commemorating such a vital national institution.

"As someone who admires the dedication of the young Americans who choose to start their service careers by joining the cadet wing at the Air Force Academy, I am deeply moved by this great honor."

Place and Date of Issue . . . . **U.S. Air Force Academy, CO,**
April 1, 2004

Art Director and Designer . . . . **Phil Jordan**

Photographer . . . . **Philip Handleman**

*FACING PAGE: An interior view of the remarkable Cadet Chapel.
ABOVE: Academy graduates celebrate their accomplishments. RIGHT:
In 1996, the Cadet Chapel received the 25-Year Award from the
American Institute of Architects.*

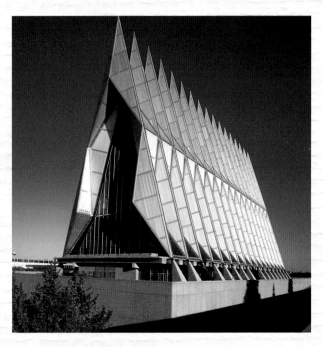

John Wayne

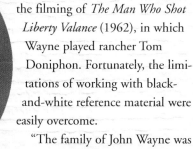

To see John Wayne on the silver screen was to behold an American film legend. Born Marion Morrison in Winterset, Iowa, in 1907, Wayne played many memorable characters, from heroic soldiers and revered figures in history to ordinary men with a deep loyalty to country and a strong commitment to justice. Exhibiting the rugged individualism associated with the American cowboy, his Western heroes became icons—and he himself became larger than life.

"John Wayne was more than just a movie star," declares stamp artist Drew Struzan, "he was a very distinct personality." No stranger to depicting heroes of the silver screen, Struzan was the natural choice to illustrate this tenth stamp in the Legends of Hollywood series. He is perhaps the best-known movie poster artist in the world, and his work has appeared on book covers, album covers, and several previous U.S. stamps.

Struzan based his painting on a black-and-white photograph of Wayne taken during the filming of *The Man Who Shot Liberty Valance* (1962), in which Wayne played rancher Tom Doniphon. Fortunately, the limitations of working with black-and-white reference material were easily overcome.

"The family of John Wayne was very helpful," he explains. "They went through his props and costumes and described them for me, even the color of his shirt and hat, and provided color photos. Apparently, some of the items you see him with in the movies weren't props; they were actually his own personal property."

Although Struzan is best known for his large-scale movie posters, he says that illustrating on the smaller scale required by the Postal Service—four to five times stamp size—doesn't cause him any trouble.

"As a professional, you just have to comprehend that something that's one inch high has certain design conceptions and parameters that need to be understood, so you keep patterns, designs, and the composition simple. You have to draw back on wanting to put the kitchen sink in. If that requires a shift in mentality and direction, that's just part of the job."

Struzan also says he's pleased that the Postal Service continues to use illustrators at a time when many designers tend to see photography as their first recourse. "People can have a very personal connection with art," he says. "Of course, I look at these things romantically, but I'm glad to see that people appreciate the artists and the work that we do."

■

Place and Date of Issue	**Los Angeles, CA, September 9, 2004**
Artist	**Drew Struzan**
Art Director and Designer	**Derry Noyes**

TOP: *A 1939 portrait of Wayne taken during the filming of* Stagecoach. LOWER LEFT: *Wayne on the job in the 1971 film* The Cowboys. FACING PAGE: *Wayne starred as an obsessed man in* The Searchers, *a brooding Western.* INSET: *The movie poster for* Stagecoach *gives John Wayne star billing.*

MEN—AND WOMEN—
ON THE LAST FRONTIER
OF WICKEDNESS!

JOHN FORD'S

STAGECOACH

JOHN WAYNE
CLAIRE TREVOR · THOMAS MITCHELL
JOHN CARRADINE
ANDY DEVINE
GEORGE BANCROFT

2
ACADEMY
AWARDS

Henry Mancini

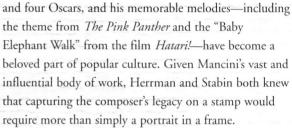

Shortly before artist Victor Stabin received the phone call to begin working on his first stamp, he had made a career-altering choice—or, at least, he thought he had.

"I had decided never to illustrate again," says Stabin. "I wanted to dedicate my life to painting." He laughs when he remembers how quickly that changed. "Of course, as soon as I said that, Carl Herrman called me about Mancini."

Carl Herrman, the Postal Service art director who discovered some of Stabin's poster work in a Society of Illustrators awards book, knew that the artist would be perfect for a stamp that needed to incorporate many different elements.

"Victor is a gifted oil painter. He's good at lively portraits but also exceptionally skilled at image manipulation on a computer. He was thrilled to get my call and quickly rattled off his favorite Mancini compositions."

One of the most successful music composers in the history of television and film, Henry Mancini left a rich legacy of catchy TV themes, hit songs, and unforgettable film scores. Mancini's awards included 20 Grammys

and four Oscars, and his memorable melodies—including the theme from *The Pink Panther* and the "Baby Elephant Walk" from the film *Hatari!*—have become a beloved part of popular culture. Given Mancini's vast and influential body of work, Herrman and Stabin both knew that capturing the composer's legacy on a stamp would require more than simply a portrait in a frame.

"Carl wanted a design that said 'cinema,'" says Stabin. "I tried a wide range of designs, probably around twenty, but the artwork really started to come together only when we put Mancini in front of a movie screen."

After Stabin had completed his portrait and the movie-theater frame, Herrman saw fit to add a few jazzy details. "At the suggestion of the Citizens' Stamp Advisory Committee, we included a partial list of Mancini's musical scores behind him, like rolling credits," he says. "And then, because the *Pink Panther* theme was one of his most memorable scores, we placed a tiny image of the cartoon character in the foreground. With those final changes, the design really came to life."

Stabin, who recently moved from New York to rural Pennsylvania, says that despite the Mancini stamp and other forthcoming Postal Service projects, he has indeed found time to pursue painting. He's also amused when he considers how the issuance of this stamp will cause a larger local stir than if he still lived in New York.

"I now live in a small town," he says, "so when I go to the post office and say, 'I did that stamp,' everyone is going to hear about it."

■

Place and Date of Issue . . . . **Los Angeles, CA, April 13, 2004**
Art Director and Designer . . . . **Carl T. Herrman**
Artist . . . . **Victor Stabin**

TOP LEFT: Mancini with a score stretched out before him. FACING PAGE: Mancini's many honors and awards included twenty Grammys and four Oscars. INSET: For the recording Our Man in Hollywood, *Mancini conducted film music composed by himself and others.* Days of Wine and Roses *represents one of his many collaborations with Blake Edwards.*

Lewis & Clark

Art director Phil Jordan laughs when he recalls the creation of the Lewis & Clark stamps and prestige booklet.

"The end results are brilliant," he says, "but when we started the journey the outcome was not at all certain—and sometimes it feels like it lasted as long as the mission of the Corps of Discovery!"

As the artist behind twelve previous stamps, designer Michael J. Deas felt that stamps commemorating the bicentennial of the beginning of Lewis and Clark's famous voyage needed to honor history through their designs as well.

"I've always loved old-fashioned stamps like the ones created during the 1920s, engraved with embellishments," he says. "I thought that look was due for a revival, and Phil very generously gave me plenty of latitude."

Deas adds that creating these stamps presented significant artistic challenges.

"You'd think there'd be great potential for epic scenes showing Lewis and Clark together," he says, "but the concept is problematic. The two men split up pretty frequently, so there were very few sites where they were actually together in a panoramic setting that was suitably majestic and would be historically accurate to depict on the stamp. In the end, I chose to depict them on a promontory as they surveyed a scenic landscape."

To create compelling portraits of the two men, Deas decided early on that copying existing artwork was simply not an option.

"I knew that I wanted to create fresh and original

Place and Date of Issue . . . . **Hartford, IL, May 14, 2004**

Art Director . . . . **Phil Jordan**

Artist and Designer . . . . **Michael J. Deas**

LEFT: Dark Butte on the Missouri River in Montana, one of many stunning views in the wilderness explored by Lewis and Clark.

paintings in the style of a painter from that period," he says. "Charles Peale painted famous portraits of Lewis and Clark, but they've been reproduced *ad infinitum.* However, I've always been fond of Gilbert Stuart and his portraits; he was alive during the time of Lewis and Clark and I greatly admire his work. So I took existing portraits and combined them to create new, authentic pictures—a new third portrait of each explorer in the style of Gilbert Stuart."

Jordan has worked with Deas on numerous previous stamps, but he relates one incident that confirmed his respect for the artist's eye for detail and the faithful research underlying Deas's work.

"Michael completed the two portraits pretty early on," Jordan says, "so during much of the design process they sat on my work table, looking down upon the third stamp and the constantly evolving prestige booklet.

"Late in the process, I bought a copy of James Holmberg's book *Dear Brother,* which compiles the letters of William Clark to his brother Jonathan. As I thumbed through the book, I came face-to-face with what I thought was Michael's portrait of Clark—but it was, in fact, a photograph of Clark's eldest son, Meriwether Lewis Clark, who was said to bear a strong resemblance to his father.

"I had never questioned the spiritual fidelity of Michael's portraits, but it was nice to see the literal fidelity confirmed as well."

■

ABOVE: At the White Cliffs of the Missouri, Lewis wrote of "seens of visionary inchantment." RIGHT: Lewis and Clark collected flora and fauna new to the science of the day. FACING PAGE: A detail of the beautiful artwork created for the Postal Service by Michael J. Deas.

American Choreographers

The choreographers honored on these stamps excelled at transforming motion into art. Through their efforts, the United States emerged as a serious presence on the international dance scene during the 20th century, with works that ranged from ballet and modern dance to musicals for theater and film.

The versatility of their extraordinary achievements helped to make them American legends—but, as art director Ethel Kessler learned, applying a consistent design across all four stamps while allowing each choreographer's individuality to shine presented an interesting challenge.

"A project such as this one needs to be sensitive to horizontal and vertical formats," she says, explaining the many questions that run through a designer's mind while working on a complex project. "What if we find the perfect image, but it's the wrong orientation and doesn't fit? Do we change the others, or look for the next-perfect image? What if it's the right format, but the wrong dance sequence? We had to keep looking until all of the elements fell into place."

One of the leading choreographers of his era, ALVIN AILEY (1931-1989) helped to popularize dance in America with works that frequently incorporated elements of modern dance, ballet, and jazz infused with the blues, Negro spirituals, and aspects of the African-American experience. Taken in 1988, a studio portrait of Ailey appears on this stamp alongside a 2000 photograph showing members of Alvin Ailey American Dance Theater performing *Revelations*. Drawing on Ailey's childhood experiences, *Revelations* is a groundbreaking work that celebrates the cultural heritage of African Americans, which Ailey described as "sometimes sorrowful, sometimes jubilant, but always hopeful."

GEORGE BALANCHINE (1904-1983) created more than 200 ballets, including *The Nutcracker* (1954) and *Square Dance* (1957). The portrait of Balanchine shown on this stamp was taken by his wife, the ballet dancer Tanaquil Le Clercq. The photograph of dancers with their backs to the camera was made circa 1970 and shows Karin von Aroldingen and other corps members of New York City Ballet in *Serenade*, the first ballet created in the U.S. by Balanchine, and the first important work of ballet ever made for American dancers.

Place and Date of Issue . . . . **Newark, NJ, May 4, 2004**

Art Director . . . . **Ethel Kessler**

Designers . . . . **Ethel Kessler and Greg Berger**

LOWER LEFT: *Members of the New York City Ballet perform George Balanchine's* Serenade.
FACING PAGE: *Members of Alvin Ailey American Dance Theater perform* Revelations.

MARTHA GRAHAM (1894-1991) is considered the principal founder of modern dance in America. Unlike previous choreographers, Graham based her work not on a pre-existing movement vocabulary but on the individual dancer's unique way of moving. An acknowledged genius in the world of dance, she choreographed more than 180 works in her lifetime, including *Appalachian Spring* (1944), and her style is still recognized as revolutionary. This stamp features a photograph of Graham taken in 1940 that shows her performing in *Letter to the World*, a dance-drama based on the life and work of Emily Dickinson, alongside a portrait taken in 1935.

With so much visual information to combine and assimilate for each stamp, Kessler describes the design process as a careful choreographing of research, color, and visual experimentation that is an art unto itself.

"It's the mystery of stamp design," she says. "Getting the subject down to its essence, being aware of what communicates at stamp size, and making sure that all of these images contribute to each other are all part of the intuitive and psychological design process that make this art such a challenge."

The work of AGNES DE MILLE (1905-1993) bridged the worlds of ballet and the Broadway musical, and her pioneering choreography for musicals such as *Oklahoma!* helped transform the musical into a serious American art form. Her genius lay in her ability to blend the language of classical ballet, the expressive quality of modern dance, and the traditions of American folk dancing to create superior choreographic entertainment that appealed to a broad public. This stamp features a photographic portrait of de Mille made in 1936 alongside a photograph of her dancing in 1944.

FACING PAGE: An acknowledged genius in the world of dance, Martha Graham choreographed more than 180 works in her lifetime. TOP LEFT: The choreography of Agnes de Mille helped transform the musical into a serious American art form. RIGHT: The work of Martha Graham has profoundly influenced contemporary choreographers.

Isamu Noguchi 1904–1988

37
USA

Isamu Noguchi 1904–1988

37
USA

Isamu Noguchi 1904–1988

37
USA

Isamu Noguchi 1904–1988

Isamu Noguchi 1904–1988

Isamu Noguchi

"Everything is sculpture," Japanese-American sculptor Isamu Noguchi once said. "Any material, any idea without hindrance born into space, I consider sculpture." With works ranging from portraits and abstract sculpture to graceful meditation gardens and sprawling landscapes, Noguchi expanded the very definition of sculpture. His approach, which merged Eastern and Western artistic influences, changed the face of American art.

For this stamp pane to commemorate Noguchi on the 100th anniversary of the year of his birth, art director Derry Noyes recalled not only her strong affection for the sculptor's work, but also an important personal experience: a memorable and illuminating meeting with Noguchi more than two decades earlier.

"In 1980, I designed a brochure, logo, maps, and a number of other graphic elements for an international sculpture conference in Washington, D.C.," Noyes explains. "Noguchi was the honorary chair and an exhibitor. We had lunch and spent a while discussing his work. Because I talked to him and saw him alongside his own sculpture, I found myself with a stronger understanding of the amazing things he was doing."

Remembering her experience designing the Alexander Calder stamps in 1998, Noyes knew that portraying sculpture at stamp size was often a difficult task.

"I wanted to show the breadth of Noguchi's work," she says. Noguchi deliberately blurred the line between art and design by creating furniture, theater sets, and other useful objects, so Noyes wanted to make sure the stamps captured as many aspects of his work as possible, from the abstract to the representational and from the functional to the purely artistic.

"I was thrilled to be able to show an Akari lamp, because he was so famous for those," she says, "and I think it's important for the public to see it alongside a very accessible portrait sculpture and some of his other, more abstract works. I think you really get a sense of Noguchi's range, as well as his eye for detail."

After much experimentation with color photographs and several design revisions, Noyes discovered the perfect way to capture the detail and textures of Noguchi's work: by using black-and-white photos.

"The black and white, and the gray tones in between, make you focus on the objects rather than be distracted by color," she explains. "It's more soothing, and it really brings out the dimensions and textures of the objects."

The resulting five stamps highlight the work of a masterful artist whose creations prompt even the most casual viewer to pause and examine them further.

"My hope," says Noyes, "is that people will see these stamps and understand that his work really speaks to a broad range of human experience."

■

Place and Date of Issue **Long Island City, NY, May 18, 2004**

Art Director and Designer . . . . **Derry Noyes**

TOP RIGHT: Noguchi positions his Skyviewing Sculpture *in a photograph taken circa 1969.*
CENTER: Noguchi's sculpture Black Sun *was influenced by frequent visits to ancient sites.*

Reproduced with permission of The Isamu Noguchi Foundation, Inc., New York.

National World War II Memorial

graph mock-ups of various details, like the wreaths and the columns, which were being erected full-size on the grounds for the final approval of the memorial committee."

Paine adds that helping to create artwork showing places before they've been built is a skill he honed while working with the National Geographic Society.

"We used to depict World's Fair sites well in advance of their construction," he says. "Often they were vast aerial views, and we could only hope that the end result resembled our artwork. I felt some of those same concerns working on this stamp."

As it turns out, Paine and Engeman were pleased to find that their visit to the construction site was time well spent.

"I recently saw a photograph of the nearly completed memorial in *The Washington Post*," Paine says proudly. "It looks great, and I think the stamp art is a good match."

Some artists are commissioned to depict people or scenes that no longer exist. For this stamp, artist Tom Engeman had an entirely different problem: He had to depict a memorial that hadn't even been built yet.

"The memorial was barely a scratch in the dirt when I was given the assignment," says Engeman, who visited the construction site on the National Mall in Washington, D.C., with art director Howard Paine. "Howard and I teamed up to photograph a scale model that was housed in a trailer on the construction site. We needed to document a variety of viewpoints and angles to determine which way the shadows fell on the memorial and other key details."

Dedicated on May 29, 2004, the memorial honors the 16 million Americans who served in the armed forces during the war and the millions more who supported them on the home front. Incorporated into the memorial is a beautiful plaza encircled by 56 pillars adorned with bronze wreaths to celebrate the unity of the nation during the war. But two years earlier, when Engeman and Paine visited during the early stages of construction, what they found was, in Paine's words, "one big mud-hole."

"Fortunately," says Engeman, "we were able to photo-

Place and Date of Issue . . . . . . **Washington, D.C., May 29, 2004**

Art Director and Designer . . . . **Howard E. Paine**

Artist . . . . **Tom Engeman**

ABOVE: A view of the National World War II Memorial. RIGHT: A crowd celebrates in Times Square on May 7, 1945.
FACING PAGE: An artist's rendering of the Atlantic Arch and Plaza at the memorial.

The Art of Disney Friendship

Since the big-screen debut of Mickey Mouse in 1928, Disney artists have worked with one purpose: to create characters and stories that speak to our emotions. For these new stamps, the U.S. Postal Service teamed up with Disney to celebrate the idea of friendship, relying on some familiar faces—and several behind-the-scenes talents as well.

"We started with friendship because it's such a strong recurring theme in Disney films," says Brian Siegel, who oversaw the team that created this first of three planned stamp panes. "To convey the Disney values of family, laughter, and heart, we decided to create moments that show the characters' relationships and what they've meant to so many generations."

From hundreds of characters, the team chose several to represent four distinct types of friendship. Mickey and his pals are the perfect fun-loving group; Pinocchio and Jiminy Cricket exemplify a mentoring relationship; Bambi and Thumper represent childhood best friends; and Mufasa and Simba show the powerful bond between parent and child.

"We wanted to show the characters' interactions clearly," says Dave Pacheco, whose role as Creative Director was to formulate the initial concepts. Pacheco points out that the varying scales of the different characters presented a challenge, and fitting Mickey, Donald, and Goofy into the small space of a single postage stamp required a clever concept to capture their essential personalities.

"My inspiration came from those automatic photo booths where friends squeeze in and jockey for position," he says. "Mickey has the best placement, Goofy doesn't mind being in back, and Donald is pushing to the front as usual."

Once Pacheco formulated the concepts, Brian Siegel needed to find the right Disney artist who could bring these stamps to life.

"Peter Emmerich was the perfect choice," says Siegel. "He's a talented young artist with tremendous love and respect for the characters."

Emmerich says that once he was presented with the initial concepts, he had some interesting creative choices to make.

"My biggest challenge was giving Dave's concepts form and volume without losing their spontaneity," he says. "I tend to work in very vivid color, but I toned it down for a more realistic feeling. I tried to express emotion through the rendering of the characters' eyes, and I concentrated less on texture and more on the light reflecting off them. For Bambi and Thumper, I used subtle blues to enhance the image and create a warm moment."

Emmerich admits that the Bambi and Thumper stamp is probably his favorite, but he is confident that all four designs will convey a sense of the warmth and support that make friendships so rewarding.

"I think that's the image I like best," he says, "but I hope each one will mean something special to everyone who uses these stamps." ∎

Place and Date of Issue . . . . **Anaheim, CA, June 23, 2004**

Art Director and Designer . . . . **Terrence W. McCaffrey**

Artist . . . . **Peter Emmerich**

ABOVE: *Disney artist Peter Emmerich, immersed in his work.*

2004 Olympic Games
Athens, Greece

The runners were there at the beginning.

The first recorded Olympic Games took place in the Greek city of Olympia in 776 B.C. and subsequently were held every four years for nearly 12 centuries. It all started with a single footrace called the stade, and as thousands of athletes convene upon historic Athens in 2004 for the games of the XXVIII Olympiad, this stamp recognizes the ancient origins of the Olympic tradition.

"The idea was to create a graphic that resembled the Attic vase paintings of Greece," says stamp artist Lonnie Busch, who created the Greetings From America stamps in 2002. After developing artistic collages for a pane of 50 stamps, Busch found that this new challenge—a single image to encapsulate the idea of the Olympic Games returning to Greece—demanded significant research as well.

"After finding as many images of vases as possible, I tried to capture the feel in an updated version," he explains. The result is a stylized depiction of a Greek runner that resembles a scene from an ancient black-figure vase. A classical design known as a meander or a key pattern, which borders the top and bottom of the stamp, helped Busch and art director Richard Sheaff meet an even larger design challenge.

"That challenge," says Busch, "was to make the image flow across the sheet of stamps." Sheaff wanted the runner, border, and background to merge into the adjoining stamps on either side, giving the appearance of a footrace when they appeared in horizontal rows on the stamp pane. Red versions of the main figure on either side of the main runner created the desired effect, and the stamp was complete.

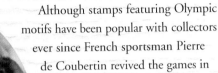

Although stamps featuring Olympic motifs have been popular with collectors ever since French sportsman Pierre de Coubertin revived the games in Athens in 1896, Busch says that he wasn't intimidated by the world-wide interest in the games or the long tradition of Olympic-themed stamps. Instead, he focused on the task at hand: capturing the idea of the Olympic Games in a single piece of art.

"In a way, that gave me freedom and protection," he says, "leaving the image fresher." His design honors all modern Olympians while acknowledging the small band of runners whose determination and competitive spirit has resonated for centuries.

Place and Date of Issue . . . . **Philadelphia, PA, June 9, 2004**
Art Director and Designer . . . . **Richard Sheaff**
Artist . . . .**Lonnie Busch**

FACING PAGE: An Olympic swimmer in training. TOP CENTER: Olympic runners burst out of the blocks. ABOVE: The Acropolis, Athens.

R. Buckminster Fuller

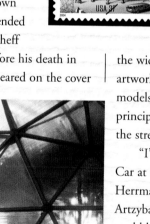

R. Buckminster Fuller looked at the world through brilliant, imaginative eyes. In his varied yet always interconnected roles as inventor, architect, engineer, designer, geometrician, cartographer, and philosopher, Fuller enlightened millions of people with his comprehensive perspective on the world's problems and the innovative solutions he developed.

"Fuller was a man ahead of his time," says art director Carl T. Herrman, who faced the daunting task of portraying Fuller's accomplishments, as well as his unique vision, in the space of a stamp. After experimenting with a variety of artistic approaches—including hexagonal stamps that resembled one of Fuller's most famous inventions, the geodesic dome—Herrman opted to use artwork that was, in its own way, as innovative as the man himself.

Early in his research, he had come across a startling and unusual portrait of Fuller by artist Boris Artzybasheff. Known for highly imaginative paintings that blended human and machine imagery, Artzybasheff created more than 200 *Time* covers before his death in 1965. His portrait of Fuller, which appeared on the cover of the magazine on January 10, 1964, reflects Fuller's belief in the potential of efficient design to improve human lives by portraying him with a head shaped like a geodesic dome.

Based on Fuller's synergetic geometry, his lifelong exploration of nature's principles of design, the geodesic dome is a lightweight, cost-effective and easy-to-assemble shelter that can withstand extremely harsh conditions. Fuller's revolutionary discoveries about balancing tension and compression forces in building led him to patent the geodesic dome in 1954, and today his name remains synonymous with the invention.

"The illustration even shows a helicopter delivering one of Fuller's domes," says Herrman, who enthusiastically points out the wide range of inventions featured on Artzybasheff's artwork, including the 4D Apartment House, several models that reflect some of the geometric and structural principles that Fuller discovered, and Herrman's favorite: the streamlined, sharp-turning Dymaxion™ Car.

"I've admired Fuller since seeing his Dymaxion Car at the Museum of Modern Art during the 1960s," Herrman says, "and I used to have an original Boris Artzybasheff *Time* cover hanging in my office. I never could have imagined someday combining Fuller and Artzybasheff on a postage stamp, but it was a marriage of two innovators, and the result is a fitting tribute to one of America's greatest thinkers."

◼

Place and Date of Issue . . . . **Stanford, CA, July 12, 2004**
Art Director and Designer . . . . **Carl T. Herrman**
Artist . . . . **Boris Artzybasheff**

LOWER LEFT: *This stamp honoring Fuller coincides with the 50th anniversary of his patent for the geodesic dome.* TOP RIGHT: *Workers swarm over the top of a geodesic dome.* FACING PAGE: *Fuller spent much of his life discovering and understanding the design principles found in nature.*

James Bald

James Baldwin

Stamp artists enjoy considerable freedom in their work and often take fresh approaches to commemorate a wide range of influential subjects. However, when Thomas Blackshear II began his portrait of James Baldwin, the 20th honoree in the Literary Arts series, he found that the creative process required a clear acknowledgement of tradition as well.

"I looked at the other Literary Arts stamps," says Blackshear. "I had to make sure my painting matched the highly detailed nature of the series and fit the style of the previous stamps."

As one of the foremost American writers of the 20th century, James Baldwin explored various subjects, including race relations, the arts, and love, in works that always showed his strong moral conscience. His writing made him a leading intellectual figure during the years of the civil rights movement, and important books such as *The Fire Next Time* eloquently articulated the complexities of race relations in America.

To commemorate this highly prolific author, Blackshear created a portrait based on a black-and-white photograph taken around 1960. The stamp background evokes Baldwin's semi-autobiographical first novel, *Go Tell It on the Mountain*, which is set in Harlem.

"It was an interesting challenge to create a portrait that fits well with a detailed street scene," says Blackshear. "Showing the detail in the background without having it overwhelm the portrait wasn't easy to do."

As the artist for nearly 30 U.S. stamps since 1987, including Classic Movie Monsters and several Black Heritage commemoratives, Blackshear brought his extensive experience with "working small" to the James Baldwin stamp—even though his studio is a busy place these days.

"I don't usually have much time for illustration assignments anymore," he says, citing his popular series of religious prints and a best-selling collection of figurines, "but I enjoy doing stamps. They're really enjoyable projects, and I always manage to find time to work on them."

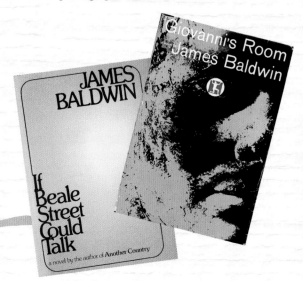

Place and Date of Issue	**New York, NY, July 23, 2004**
Art Director and Designer	**Phil Jordan**
Artist	**Thomas Blackshear II**

FACING PAGE: *Baldwin in New York, 1948.* TOP RIGHT: *Baldwin seated on a Paris terrace around 1960.*
ABOVE: *Editions of two of Baldwin's acclaimed works.*

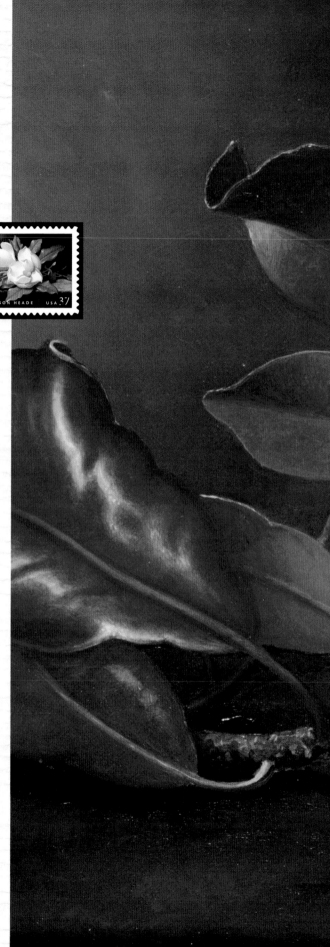

Martin Johnson Heade

S ince its debut in 2001, the American Treasures series has highlighted stunning examples of American fine arts and crafts. Always looking for beautiful artwork to appear on stamps, art director Derry Noyes found a painting that she knew was perfect for the series, *Giant Magnolias on a Blue Velvet Cloth*, in the collection of the National Gallery of Art in Washington, D.C.

"Considering where we've been with this series," says Noyes, "from the textiles of Amish Quilts to the birds of John James Audubon and the women and children of Mary Cassatt, it seemed the right time to introduce lovely flowers by one of the great American artists, Martin Johnson Heade."

Heade was born August 11, 1819, in rural Lumberville, Pennsylvania. From the early 1860s—when he began to develop his individual style—to the early 1880s, he painted coastal and inland views, floral still lifes, and tropical landscapes with hummingbirds and flowers. Forgotten for decades after his death in 1904, Heade was rediscovered in the 1940s and became the subject of major retrospectives in 1969 and 1999.

Mindful that millions of people will enjoy the work of this talented and innovative artist on their cards and letters, Noyes points out that of all Heade's works, *Giant Magnolias* was ideally suited to appear on a stamp.

"I've had my eye on his paintings for a long time," she says, "but most of them are just too dark and detailed to hold up at stamp size. This one has enough silhouette, contrast, and color—and the subject is attractive to all."

Place and Date of Issue . . . . . . **Sacramento, CA, August 12, 2004**

Art Director and Designer . . . .**Derry Noyes**

Existing Art by . . . . **Martin Johnson Heade**

RIGHT: *This detail of a magnolia painting by Martin Johnson Heade shows the intricacy with which he approached his work.*

USS *Constellation*

For this stamp to commemorate the 150th anniversary of the USS *Constellation*, art director Howard Paine was careful to consider not only the history of the venerable sailing ship, but also the needs and interests of traditional philatelists.

"This stamp is for the serious collector," says Paine. "Philatelists like engraved stamps, and that traditional design method is well suited to a rich historical subject such as this one."

The last all-sail-powered warship built by the U.S. Navy and the last Civil War–era naval vessel still afloat, *Constellation* was constructed at Gosport Navy Yard near Norfolk, Virginia, and launched on August 26, 1854. *Constellation* actively served the nation for nearly 100 years, including a stint as relief flagship for the U.S. Atlantic Fleet and Battleship Division Five during World War II. Today the ship is a floating museum anchored in the Inner Harbor at Baltimore, where it has been meticulously restored to its original 1854 configuration.

Given the numerous reconfigurations of *Constellation* during its 150-year history, Paine was especially concerned with portraying minute details as accurately as possible. He became particularly aware of the need for careful scrutiny when he decided to base the stamp engraving on a circa 1893 print in the collection of the U.S. Naval Historical Center.

"The experts who looked at the photograph told us that it showed the *Constellation* at a time when the ship was painted differently than it is now," he explains. "In particular, the gun ports along the side weren't quite right, so I asked Richard Schlecht, the consummate maritime artist, to touch up the photo digitally before we used it as the basis for the engraving."

Schlecht, who has helped to create more than 20 previous U.S. postage stamps, made the necessary changes to the image of the *Constellation*, and Paine proceeded to create a commemorative that embodies a classic approach to stamp design.

"It was vital to keep it simple, and square, and strong," says Paine. "This is a serious, traditional subject, and I wanted to make sure that the design reflected that."

■

Place and Date of Issue	**Baltimore, MD, June 30, 2004**
Art Director and Designer	**Howard E. Paine**

FACING PAGE: Constellation *docked at Portsmouth, New Hampshire, during the 1880s.* UPPER RIGHT: *This 1862 painting by Tomaso DeSimone shows* Constellation *entering the harbor in Naples, Italy.* LOWER RIGHT: *An 1856 painting, also by DeSimone, depicts* Constellation *in Naples on its first cruise.*

ART OF THE AMERICAN INDIAN

2004
Mimbres bowl USA37

2004
Kutenai parfleche USA37

2004
Tlingit sculptures USA37

2004
Ho-Chunk bag USA37

2004
Seminole doll USA37

2004
Mississippian effigy USA37

2004
Acoma pot USA37

2004
Navajo weaving USA37

2004
Seneca carving USA37

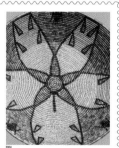

2004
Luiseño basket USA37

Art of the
American Indian

For these new stamps honoring American Indian art and design, art director Richard Sheaff knew that telling the story of some often-overlooked artifacts would require a unique approach—as well as the largest canvasses available to a stamp designer.

"They're the first jumbo stamps the Postal Service has issued in a while," Sheaff explains. "We originally started with a design that featured 20 stamps, but when the Citizens' Stamp Advisory Committee reviewed it, the members commented that they wished they could see the objects in greater detail. In response, we reduced the number of stamps, but we made the remaining designs substantially larger—which, as it turns out, finally did justice to the beauty and workmanship of the objects we selected."

In the context of their everyday lives, American Indians created a wide range of utilitarian, spiritual, and commercial objects, including those featured on this stamp pane.
Keeping in mind that the stamps present artifacts from the 11th century A.D. to circa 1969, Sheaff took great care to ensure that each object was shown in a way that encouraged thoughtfulness on the part of the viewer.

"I didn't want the stamp pane to resemble a museum catalog," he says, "which is why we made an effort to vary the ways that we showed the objects. On some of these stamps, the nature of each object is pretty clear: the Seminole doll, the Acoma pot, and the Tlingit sculptures are easily identifiable. In other cases, such as the Mimbres bowl or the Ho-Chunk bag, we've zoomed in

Place and Date of Issue . . . . **Santa Fe, NM, August 21, 2004**
Art Director and Designer . . . . **Richard Sheaff**

FACING PAGE: Humans, animals, and other forms adorn a wall called the Newspaper Rock in Indian Creek State Park, Utah.
ABOVE RIGHT: A Hopi woman decorates pottery, circa 1900. RIGHT: A late 19th-century Sioux dress decorated with beadwork.
INSET RIGHT: A Navajo woman in New Mexico weaves a rug on a loom.

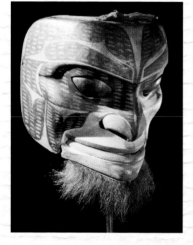

very closely, and what the stamp shows is an almost abstract detail that communicates the artistry of the object. This variation makes for a visually striking stamp pane, and I think it helps convey a broad span of time and the differences between the various cultures."

Issued to coincide with the opening of the National Museum of the American Indian in Washington, D.C., this stamp pane features objects from the museum's collection as well as artifacts from museums around the country, suggesting regional differences that Sheaff believes are vital to understanding American Indian art.

"We tried to represent various geographic areas," he says. "For example, the stamp pane includes a sandstone effigy from Tennessee, a woven textile from New Mexico, and a bag from the Great Lakes and Central Plains area. Of course, it's not possible to represent every region of the country on ten stamps, but the differences between these objects should convey an appreciation of the artistry and diversity."

Sheaff adds that beyond the opportunity to put a beautiful stamp on an envelope, the Art of the American Indian stamp pane may serve an educational purpose as well.

"The tradition of American Indian art is long and complex," he says, "and these stamps may introduce quite a few people to the subject. It's satisfying to be a part of a project that moves past stereotypes and gets people to think about the personalities and history behind these creations."

◼

ABOVE: A Tsimshian dance mask. INSET RIGHT: A Chippewa headdress. FACING PAGE: Edward S. Curtis took this fascinating photograph of American Indians in 1908. INSET: A totem pole featuring an eagle motif from British Columbia, Canada.

CLOUDSCAPES

37 USA	**37 USA**	**37 USA**	**37 USA**	**37 USA**
Cirrus radiatus	Cirrostratus fibratus	Cirrocumulus undulatus	Cumulonimbus mammatus	Cumulonimbus incus
37 USA	**37 USA**	**37 USA**	**37 USA**	**37 USA**
Altocumulus stratiformis	Altostratus translucidus	Altocumulus undulatus	Altocumulus castellanus	Altocumulus lenticularis
37 USA	**37 USA**	**37 USA**	**37 USA**	**37 USA**
Stratocumulus undulatus	Stratus opacus	Cumulus humilis	Cumulus congestus	Cumulonimbus with tornado

© 2003
USPS

.37
x 15
$5.55

X1111

PLATE
POSITION

X1111

Cloudscapes

When discussing these dramatic new stamps, Howard Paine laughs at the suggestion that his head is in the clouds. In fact, he insists that he found the inspiration for Cloudscapes right here on the ground.

"Around ten years ago," he explains, "I took my boys to summer camp and saw a poster illustrating a number of clouds tacked on the wall of a porch, and I thought, 'Gee, that looks like a sheet of stamps.' I went to look at it more closely and the thought occurred to me: 'Well, why not a sheet of stamps?' I realized the subject could be informative as well as attractive."

Working with meteorologists, researchers, and cloud photographers, Paine created a design that showed fifteen stamps in three rows according to the typical altitude of each cloud. He also made sure that verso text illuminated the methods used to name and identify each cloud, and that the text included the name of a figure prominently associated with the scientific study of clouds, Sir Luke Howard.

"I read about him when I was a kid, and I really wanted to make sure that he was mentioned in the text," Paine says. "He's the person who gave clouds the names we still use, and he was a true product of his age. When everyone was classifying everything from turtles to seashells, he was classifying clouds."

Sir Luke, a chemist by trade and meteorologist by avocation, created a system for classifying clouds using Latin names that we still use today, a fact that prompts Paine to see the Cloudscapes stamps as serving dual purposes.

"I wanted to create something that was informative and attractive at the same time," he says. "These stamps offer an informed look at the world around us, and I think people can really learn from them—and they'll look beautiful on envelopes."

■

Place and Date of Issue . . . . **Milton, MA, October 4, 2004**
Art Director and Designer . . . . **Howard E. Paine**

Sickle Cell Disease
Awareness

Stamps that raise awareness of health and social issues can be some of the most difficult to design. According to art director Howard Paine, balancing the seriousness of a subject such as sickle cell disease awareness with positive, appealing artwork requires creativity, sensitivity, and above all, collaboration.

"I find that the most important decision I can make as an art director is choosing the right artist," he says, "and for this stamp I definitely chose the right artist. James Gurney is a great painter, and his work is extremely thorough."

Gurney is best known for bringing dinosaurs back to life in works ranging from his acclaimed *Dinotopia* books to the popular World of Dinosaurs stamp pane issued in 1997, but he was enthusiastic about the opportunity to portray an important health issue that affects people in the here and now.

"I was honored to take on the challenge," he says, "but I knew it wouldn't be easy to visualize an incurable hereditary blood disease in a way that would be inviting and interesting. Unfortunately, the image that comes readily to mind for most people is a microscope slide showing elongated red blood cells alongside normal round cells."

"We did try that approach," Paine adds, "but showing actual sickle cells simply didn't work. It was far too clinical. That's when I remembered the main lesson from my years at *National Geographic*: Human interest is a crucial element in any picture."

With that directive in mind, Paine and Gurney began to develop new ideas that focused on the concept of a parent's love for a child. "The message then becomes a positive one," Gurney explains. "It reminds at-risk parents to test early to find out if they have the disease or are a carrier of the inherited sickle cell trait." Using models as the basis for his final oil painting, Gurney made sure to keep the background light and warm, with the phrase "Test Early for Sickle Cell" printed in understated tones. "The final design is very satisfying," concludes Paine.

As researchers continue to search for a cure and experiment with more effective treatments, awareness of the disease can be a vital tool. People with sickle cell disease have special needs and require regular care to stay as healthy as possible, and their families need to be aware of special support groups devoted to helping them deal with the stress of the disease.

"This stamp has the potential to reach a wide range of people," says Gurney. "It's my hope that it will raise awareness of this very important health issue."

■

Place and Date of Issue . . . . . . **Atlanta, GA, September 29, 2004**
Art Director . . . . **Howard E. Paine**
Artist . . . . **James Gurney**

ABOVE: Sickle-shaped red blood cells block blood flow and cause damage to organs.

Moss Hart

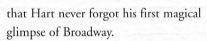

Just because stamp artists "work small" doesn't mean they work hastily. Tim O'Brien, who created stamp artwork to honor dramatist and director Moss Hart on the 100th anniversary of his birth, feels strongly that solid research always comes first.

"I was fascinated by Hart's huge presence during the golden age of theater," says O'Brien, who familiarized himself with Hart's contributions as a lyricist, playwright, and director. Hart was a theater legend, a witty and charming personality who embodied the glamor of Broadway, and O'Brien knew that portraying him properly would require an eye for detail and a thoughtful approach.

"I'm often commissioned to do portraits that are reverential," he explains, "but with Moss Hart, I wanted to get it exactly right: not too much dramatic 'stage lighting,' but a soft, general light."

Using a reference photograph made by Alfred Eisenstaedt that showed Hart in Times Square, O'Brien focused on creating the portrait in the foreground, but he also knew that the background needed to acknowledge that Hart never forgot his first magical glimpse of Broadway.

"I looked at some wonderful images of the Great White Way," O'Brien says, "but I've always felt that no one photograph can capture the essence of Broadway. I started making marquees with titles of his major works, and then I moved these sketches around until I felt confident I had it." O'Brien's stamp art includes the glittering titles of *My Fair Lady*, the musical that won Hart a Tony Award for direction; the Hollywood satire *Once in a Lifetime*; and the witty backstage comedy *Light Up the Sky*. Appropriately, O'Brien also included another name in lights: Moss Hart's own.

"I enjoyed creating this little homage to such a giant," says O'Brien, who was thrilled to learn that Hart's widow, Kitty Carlisle Hart, loved his painting. "In the end, that personal affirmation is quite a gift."

■

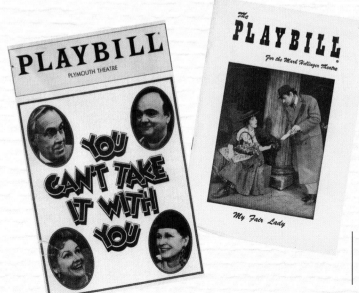

Place and Date of Issue . . . . **New York, NY, October 24, 2004**

Art Director and Designer . . . . **Ethel Kessler**

Artist . . . . **Tim O'Brien**

TOP: *Hart talks with dancer and choreographer Roland Petit on the set of the film* Hans Christian Andersen. LEFT: *Two program covers show some of the talented performers in Hart's productions.* FACING PAGE: *Moss Hart at home in Times Square in 1959.*

SIXTH IN A SERIES

PACIFIC CORAL REEF

NATURE OF AMERICA

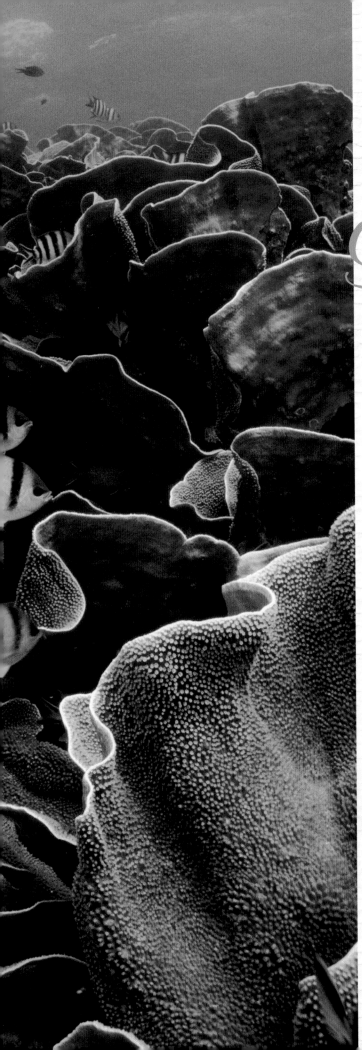

Pacific Coral Reef

Since 1999, the Nature of America series has promoted appreciation of major plant and animal communities in North America. This year, the series expands to include a coral reef near Guam, a U.S. territory in the western Pacific Ocean. A vivid painting by series artist John D. Dawson takes viewers deep within a coral reef, a structure built up by tiny organisms called coral polyps that secrete calcium carbonate.

Dawson, who lives in Hawaii, was delighted to portray the beauty and complexity of an aquatic ecosystem. However, he and his wife, Kathleen, were amused to learn that for some children, the fascinating undersea world depicted on this stamp pane was already a familiar place.

"Right after I finished the Pacific Coral Reef painting," Dawson explains, "Kathleen and I were on vacation and were snorkeling with our two very young granddaughters. They had just seen the movie *Finding Nemo* and were a little obsessed. They didn't understand that here in Hawaii, we don't have clownfish. In spite of that, we continued the game of 'searching for Nemo' in all the tidal pools. What we did find was one of the co-stars of the movie: some of the small blue and black palette surgeonfish. We were all excited to see some very famous movie stars who are also in the Coral Reef art."

Dawson's work has been commissioned by the National Geographic Society, the National Park Service, and numerous other prominent organizations, and his award-winning paintings for the Nature of America series have won praise from stamp collectors and the general public alike. However, he's especially satisfied that his work passed the toughest test of all.

"It was a thrill to share the adventure with the granddaughters," says Dawson, "and now they think their grandpa is kind of cool."

■

Place and Date of Issue . . . . **Honolulu, HI, January 2, 2004**

Art Director and Designer . . . . **Ethel Kessler**

Artist . . . . **John D. Dawson**

LEFT: *Fish known as scissortail sergeants inhabit colonies of plate coral in this scene from the South Pacific.*

Hanukkah

For this new design in the Holiday Celebrations stamp series, art director Ethel Kessler was pleased to explore new ways of envisioning Hanukkah, especially since she feels an especially strong connection to the subject.

"My family has celebrated Hanukkah since long before I was born," she explains, "so it's a holiday with joyous memories for me. The symbols are simple, the story is ancient, and the holiday is a fun celebration involving food, candles, the dreidel game, and small gifts on each of the eight nights."

Kessler's familiarity with the subject meant that she was faced with an interesting challenge when she had to pare down the range of potential design approaches.

"There are so many variations of the two main symbols of the holiday, menorahs and dreidels, that it was overwhelming," she says. "I wondered: Should the stamp represent an ancient story or be a contemporary interpretation? Could it show the rich craft heritage while also representing the joy of the holiday celebration? I think that's what we accomplished with the final artwork: a blending of the two."

■

Place and Date of Issue . . . . **New York, NY, October 15, 2004**

Art Director and Designer . . . . **Ethel Kessler**

Photographer . . . . **Elise Moore**

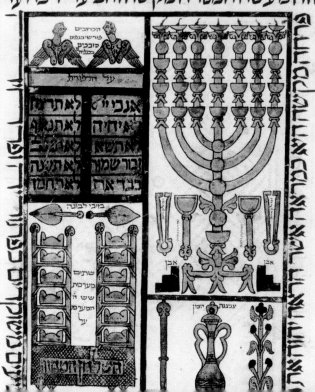

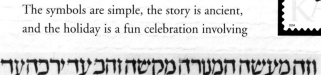

ABOVE LEFT: A beautiful hand-painted dreidel from Israel. ABOVE RIGHT: A family gathers around the menorah. LEFT: This illuminated manuscript from the beginning of the 14th century depicts several Jewish ritual objects.

Kwanzaa

To create a new design for this year's Kwanzaa stamp, the Postal Service called upon Daniel Minter, an artist who approached the subject with a confident familiarity.

"I've worked on numerous projects related to Kwanzaa," Minter explains. "A few years ago I illustrated a children's book about the subject, and I've also spoken to groups of children about the holiday. Because I've been involved with promoting Kwanzaa in a number of ways, creating artwork for the stamp felt like a very natural extension of my previous experience."

As he developed ideas for the stamp design, Minter considered the principles underlying the holiday and sought to convey them in his artwork.

"My goal was to expand upon the dimension and effect of the Nguzo Saba, the seven principles of Kwanzaa, and to reach

out to the community. I like to think of the Kwanzaa stamp as the seven virtues compressed, and that they expand once you receive the stamp in the mail."

Minter also made sure that the stamp was an interesting mingling of traditional and contemporary approaches.

"I started off by creating a black-and-white linoleum-block print," Minter explains. "I scanned that and used two different computer programs to add color. The result is half digital art, half old-fashioned print art—a combination of perspectives that I think is really appropriate to the holiday."

■

Place and Date of Issue . . . . **Chicago, IL, October 16, 2004**

Art Director and Designer . . . . **Derry Noyes**

Artist . . . . **Daniel Minter**

ABOVE RIGHT: Begun in 1966, Kwanzaa has its roots in ancient and modern African harvest celebrations. LEFT: Kwanzaa celebrates seven principles: unity, self-determination, collective work and responsibility, cooperative economics, purpose, creativity, and faith.

Holiday Ornaments and Christmas

Sally Andersen-Bruce has an eye for photographing beloved objects that look great at stamp size, from snowman figurines to antique toys. For these Holiday Ornaments stamps, she faced an interesting new challenge: the items she selected had to fit a larger concept as well.

"You're supposed to feel like you're taking an ornament out of a box each time you use one of these stamps," she explains. "For three months, I photographed all sorts of ornaments in different combinations, but I just couldn't find four that worked well together."

Fortunately, a friend with a large collection of ornaments recommended D. Blümchen & Company in Ridgewood, New Jersey, where Andersen-Bruce found inspiration in a Christmas wonderland.

"I visited their atelier, and it was a wonderful place where all of the women were decorating ornaments with little paintbrushes," she says. "While I was there, I saw an illustration in their catalog for 'Happy Santas.' I was intrigued by them, but their faces were very minimal, so I asked Diane Boyce, the president and creative director, if she could make them jollier. It took her days to repaint each face, especially since these ornaments are tiny—only around two inches high—but she did a really wonderful job, and

you can see her beautiful work on these stamps. She made their smiles bigger and rosier, she replaced the silver hangers with gold, and she even put gold leaf on the belt buckles."

Before photographing these ornaments, Andersen-Bruce placed them in custom-built boxes with fifteen types of antique paper, which recalled her own collection of Christmas ornaments.

"We have some that have been in my family for years. My grandmother made ornaments for me, and my mother picked up on the tradition as well. These special objects connect the generations. Every holiday season, they bring back wonderful memories of Christmases past."

This year, the U.S. Postal Service also recognizes Christmas with a stamp that features a detail of a tempera-on-panel *Madonna and Child* by Florentine painter Lorenzo Monaco. The panel, which dates from 1413, is part of the Samuel H. Kress Collection at the National Gallery of Art in Washington, D.C. Designed by Richard Sheaff, this stamp continues a Postal Service tradition of using fine art to adorn some of our warmest Christmas wishes.

"People react so positively to Christmas stamps," says Andersen-Bruce, who continues to photograph holiday-themed objects for future issuances. "They're great reminders of the spirit of the season." ∎

HOLIDAY ORNAMENTS

Place and Date of Issue ..... **New York, NY, November 16, 2004**

Art Director and Designer .... **Derry Noyes**

Photographer .... **Sally Andersen-Bruce**

CHRISTMAS: *MADONNA AND CHILD* BY LORENZO MONACO

Place and Date of Issue .... **New York, NY, October 14, 2004**

Art Director and Designer .... **Richard Sheaff**

FACING PAGE: This year's Holiday Ornaments stamps recall the European origins of modern depictions of Santa Claus. RIGHT: A detail from Virgin and Child, *a painting attributed to Raphael.*

Photo Credits

Cover

Giant Magnolias on a Blue Velvet Cloth, Gift of The Circle of the National Gallery of Art in Commemoration of its 10th Anniversary, Image © 2004 Board of Trustees, National Gallery of Art, Washington

Introduction

Page 4
   © Bettmann/CORBIS

Page 5
   © Alex Gotfryd/CORBIS

Lunar New Year: Year of the Monkey

Page 6
   (left) Private Collection/Bridgeman Art Library
   (upper right) © Historical Picture Archive/CORBIS

Page 7
   Painting by Lizzie Riches, Portal Gallery, London/Bridgeman Art Library

Black Heritage: Paul Robeson

Page 8
   Sasha/Getty Images

Page 9
   (center and lower left) Courtesy Photofest

Love: Candy Hearts

Pages 10–11
   © Lyn Hughes/CORBIS

Theodor Seuss Geisel

Pages 12–13
   All artwork and photograph of Theodor Seuss Geisel used with permission of Dr. Seuss Properties™ & © Dr. Seuss Enterprises, L.P. All rights reserved.

Garden Blossoms

Page 14
   (top) © Claudia Kunin/CORBIS
   (bottom) © Royalty-Free/CORBIS

Page 15
   © Royalty-Free/CORBIS

U.S. Air Force Academy

Page 16
   © Jim Richardson/CORBIS

Page 17
   (top) © Joseph Sohm; Visions of America/CORBIS
   (bottom) © Dave G. Houser/CORBIS

Legends of Hollywood: John Wayne

Page 18
   (top) Ned Scott/MPTV.net
   (bottom) David Sutton/MPTV.net

Page 19
   (full page) THE SEARCHERS © Warner Bros. Entertainment Inc. All Rights Reserved. Photograph courtesy Photofest
   (inset) Courtesy of the Academy of Motion Picture Arts and Sciences

Henry Mancini

Page 20
   (upper left) © Steve Banks 1980, photograph appears courtesy of the Henry Mancini Estate
   (lower left and lower right) Artwork courtesy MGM

Page 21
   (full page) Photograph appears courtesy of the Henry Mancini Estate
   (right inset) Courtesy Photofest
   (left inset) Used courtesy of the RCA Records Label

Lewis & Clark

Pages 22–23
   © Wayne Mumford, www.lewisandclarkpictures.com

Page 24
   (upper left) © Wayne Mumford, www.lewisandclarkpictures.com
   (insets) Courtesy North Wind Picture Archives

Pages 24–25
   Artwork by Michael J. Deas © U.S. Postal Service

American Choreographers

Page 26
   (lower left) David Lindner/Landov
   (top) Jerome Robbins Dance Division, The New York Public Library for the Performing Arts, Astor, Lenox and Tilden Foundations
   (lower right) Photograph by George Platt Lynes, courtesy Jerome Robbins Dance Division, The New York Public Library for the Performing Arts, Astor, Lenox and Tilden Foundations

Page 27
   Andrew Eccles/jbgphoto.com

Page 28
   Jerome Robbins Dance Division, The New York Public Library for the Performing Arts, Astor, Lenox and Tilden Foundations

Page 29
   (lower left) © Bettmann/CORBIS
   (lower right) © Barbara Morgan, Courtesy Jerome Robbins Dance Division, The New York Public Library for the Performing Arts, Astor, Lenox and Tilden Foundations and The Barbara Morgan Archive
   (upper right) © Bettmann/CORBIS
   (upper left) Jerome Robbins Dance Division, The New York Public Library for the Performing Arts, Astor, Lenox and Tilden Foundations

Isamu Noguchi

Page 30
   Photograph by Kaz Inouye, Courtesy The Isamu Noguchi Foundation, Inc.

Page 31
   (upper right) Courtesy The Isamu Noguchi Foundation, Inc.
   (bottom) Photograph by Michio Noguchi, Courtesy The Isamu Noguchi Foundation, Inc.

Photo Credits

National World War II Memorial
Page 32
   (upper left) © CORBIS SYGMA
   (lower right) © Bettmann/CORBIS

Page 33
   © Michael McCann, Courtesy of the American Battle
   Monuments Commission

The Art of Disney: Friendship
Pages 34–35
   All artwork and photograph of Peter Emmerich © Disney

2004 Olympic Games * Athens, Greece
Page 36
   © Reuters NewMedia Inc./CORBIS

Page 37
   (top) © Jerry Cooke/CORBIS
   (lower right) © Wolfgang Kaehler/CORBIS

R. Buckminster Fuller
Page 38
   (upper right) Howard Sochurek/Getty Images
   (lower left) © Joseph Sohm; ChromoSohm Inc./CORBIS

Page 39
   Courtesy Boston Public Library, Print Department

Literary Arts: James Baldwin
Page 40
   © Karl Bissinger, James Baldwin, New York City, 1968

Page 41
   (top) Photograph and Prints Division, Schomburg Center for
   Research in Black Culture, The New York Public Library,
   Astor, Lenox and Tilden Foundations
   (right inset) Courtesy Library of Congress
   (left inset) Courtesy, Cal Poly Pomona University Library
   Special Collections

American Treasures: Martin Johnson Heade
Pages 42–43
   © Christie's Images/CORBIS

USS *Constellation*
Page 44
   Patch Collection, Strawbery Banke Museum, Portsmouth,
   New Hampshire

Page 45
   (bottom) USS *Constellation* Museum, Baltimore, MD
   (top) US Naval Historical Center, courtesy USS *Constellation*
   Museum, Baltimore, MD

Art of the American Indian
Page 46
   © David Muench/CORBIS

Page 47
   (top) © CORBIS

   (bottom) © Christie's Images/CORBIS
   (lower right inset) © Danny Lehman/CORBIS

Page 48
   (upper left) © Werner Forman/CORBIS
   (lower right) © Bowers Museum of Cultural Art/CORBIS

Pages 48–49
   © Stapleton Collection/CORBIS

Page 49
   © Ron Watts/CORBIS

Cloudscapes
Pages 50–51
   © Royalty-Free/CORBIS

Sickle Cell Disease Awareness
Page 52
   © Images.com/CORBIS

Page 53
   (upper right) © Lester V. Bergman/CORBIS
   (lower left) © Ariel Skelley/CORBIS

Moss Hart
Page 54
   (lower left, both) Courtesy Photofest
   (upper right) Gjon Mili/Getty Images

Page 55
   Alfred Eisenstaedt/Getty Images

Nature of America: Pacific Coral Reef
Pages 56–57
   © Mark Conlin/SeaPics.com

Holiday Celebrations: Hanukkah
Page 58
   (top right) © Roy Morsch/CORBIS
   (bottom left) © Archivo Iconografico, S.A./CORBIS
   (top left) Photograph by Elise Moore/PhotoAssist, Inc.

Holiday Celebrations: Kwanzaa
Page 59
   (bottom left) Mark Adams/Getty Images
   (upper right) © Ariel Skelley/CORBIS

Holiday Ornaments and Christmas
Page 60
   (full page) © Images.com/CORBIS

Page 61
   (top) Photograph by Sally Andersen-Bruce © U.S. Postal Service
   (lower right) © Burstein Collection/CORBIS

Background on text pages
   © Getty Images

Acknowledgments

These stamps and this stamp-collecting book were produced by Stamp Services, Government Relations, United States Postal Service.

JOHN E. POTTER
Postmaster General,
Chief Executive Officer

RALPH J. MODEN
Senior Vice President,
Government Relations and Public Policy

DAVID E. FAILOR
Executive Director,
Stamp Services

Special thanks are extended to the following individuals for their contributions to the production of this book:

UNITED STATES POSTAL SERVICE

TERRENCE W. McCAFFREY
Manager, Stamp Development

CINDY L. TACKETT
Manager, Stamp Exhibitions
and Products

SONJA D. EDISON
Project Manager

HARPERCOLLINS PUBLISHERS

NICK DARRELL
Assistant Editor,
HarperResource

LUCY ALBANESE
Design Director,
General Books Group

JESSICA CHIN
Production Editor,
General Books Group

SUSAN KOSKO
Director of Production,
General Books Group

NIGHT & DAY DESIGN

TIMOTHY SHANER
Art Director, Designer

PHOTOASSIST, INC.

JEFF SYPECK
Copywriter

MIKE OWENS
Photo Editor
Rights and Permissions

GREG VARNER
Text Research and Editing

THE CITIZENS' STAMP ADVISORY COMMITTEE

DR. VIRGINIA M. NOELKE
CARY R. BRICK
MICHAEL R. BROCK
MEREDITH J. DAVIS
DAVID L. ENYON
JEAN PICKER FIRSTENBERG
SYLVIA HARRIS
I. MICHAEL HEYMAN
JOHN M. HOTCHNER
DR. C. DOUGLAS LEWIS
KARL MALDEN
RICHARD F. PHELPS
RONALD A. ROBINSON
MARUCHI SANTANA